AWAKEN
Sleeping Beauty

ISBN: 978-0-9996778-4-1 (Paper Back)

PRINTED IN THE UNITED STATES OF AMERICA

Book Design & Layout: Russell Lake - SeedStudios.com
Cover Illustration: Malika Roberts - MalikasArtAndMurals.com
Back Cover Photos: Impressions Photography- Shannon Ireland
                    On location at Drumoland Castle
Interior Illustrations: Ailbhe Cronin-Ireland - AppleBerryPress.com

First Edition April 2018

Published by:
Pogue Family Mission Society
1512 Bray Central Drive
Suite 300
McKinney, Texas 75069

AWAKEN
Sleeping Beauty

BIBLE STUDY

Judy Pogue

Bellingham Castle

Castlebellingham, Co. Louth, Ireland

TABLE OF CONTENTS

SCRIPTURES FROM DAY ONE:

DEUT   29:29
ISA   52:1-2
JER   33:3
MATT   22:37-38
PS   16:11

LEAVE A LEGACY OF CHARACTER & FAITH

NCE UPON A TIME IN A LAND FAR, FAR AWAY, THERE LIVED A PRINCESS IN A ROYAL CASTLE. HER NAME WAS SLEEPING BEAUTY…

STEP BACK IN TIME WITH ME AND SEE HOW THIS MEDIEVAL STORY TOLD IN A MODERN-DAY TEXT PERTAINS TO THE WOMEN OF TODAY…

The Lord wants you—yes, *you*—to awaken from your slumber, sister.

He wants you to wipe the sleep from your eyes and the fog from your mind and become *fully awake* to the life He has created and designed for you.

He wants the women of this world who know Him as Christ to come together to move mountains. And save lives. And to live intentionally as an example for others to follow.

He wants you to fully embrace what you are to Him—a queen to be honored, a daughter to be cherished, and a woman called to live a Christ-filled life. When you accepted the call upon your life to follow Christ, you became an ambassador for His Kingdom, fully equipped and blessed beyond measure. You received the power to impact neighbors and cities and *countries* because of your calling. You are called, dear friend.

You have everything you need for your grand and extraordinary adventure. Just one thing is asked of you to accomplish this divine calling: *awaken sleeping beauty.*

The next six weeks of your life could be *transformational.*

This study could be a *turning point* in coming to understand how immeasurably loved and valued you are by God.

The verses in these pages are *powerful*; the encouragements and perspectives offered are genuine and heartfelt and intended *for you.*

My hope is that, at the end of this study and as you work through these pages, you will feel a renewed sense of self-worth and value; that you will understand, accept, and embrace your divine calling; and that you will *wake up* to the call of God upon your heart.

You were created to impact Christ's Kingdom in ways that you *alone* are uniquely gifted to do so. *No other woman on the planet* has your divinely designed set of gifts and talents and blessings—*no one.*

It's time, dear sister. It's time to *wake up to the call of Christ upon your life.*

WAKE UP, SLEEPING BEAUTY

"Awake, awake, Zion,
clothe yourself with strength!
Put on your garments of splendor,
Jerusalem, the holy city...Shake
off your dust; rise up, sit enthroned,
Jerusalem. Free yourself from the
chains on your neck, Daughter Zion,
now a captive."

Isaiah 52:1-2

Principles to Ponder –

- ❊ The Lord wants you to awaken from your slumber and to be fully awake to the destiny He has designed for you.
- ❊ God wants you to understand you are a queen to be honored and a daughter to be cherished.

Questions to Discuss –

❊ How have so many of the women of this world fallen asleep and lost their ability to dream? How do you see this loss of fulfillment play out in their lives?

_____

_____

_____

_____

❊ What distractions do you think keep women in general from fulfilling their destiny? What distractions do you face that stand *in your way?*

_____

_____

_____

_____

_____

❀ What are the dreams God has deposited *in your heart?* What has prevented you from pursuing them? Doubt? Fear? Time? Money?

❀ What *one thing* could you do today to start dreaming and moving closer to awakening to your call? Can you think of one small step you could take every day for a week? A month? Consider how you would speak to a friend asking for your help. Now, be just as kind and compassionate to yourself as you would to them.

❀ Are you able to step forward without burdens from your past holding you back? If not, what can you do to "free yourself from the chains" that are preventing you from making progress?

"This is what the Lord says, ... 'Call to me and I will answer you and tell you great and unsearchable things you do not know.'"

—Jeremiah 33:2-3

Always Remember This –

God wants to give you freedom and give you hope for tomorrow.

Prayer –

"Father God, open my eyes and my spirit to hear your voice. Let me feel your presence and set me free from any past failures and fears. Break the chains of bondage and let me be truly free. Amen."

_____

_____

_____

_____

A Visitation from God

"You make known to me the path of life; you will fill me with joy in your presence, with eternal pleasures at your right hand."

–Psalms 16:11

Principles to Ponder –

- ✻ When you get into the presence of God, things begin to change; they *must* change.
- ✻ As a woman of Christ, you have a tremendous responsibility *and opportunity* to have strong and thriving marriage, to raise godly children, and to be an honorable example in your businesses and in your community.
- ✻ You are called to model Christ to others in all that you do *all day, every day.*

Questions to Discuss –

- ✤ What happens in your spirit when you don't take the time to pray and worship the Lord? Can you tell a difference in how your day plays out when you do and, especially, *when you don't?* What stands in your way each morning that regularly prevents you from a few moments of prayer and devotion?

_____

_____

_____

_____

_____

_____

❀ How can you (or already do) guard your heart and mind from the influences of the world? What are the biggest outside influencers that shape your thoughts and opinions about what is right? What is acceptable? What is considered politically correct? What is considered worthy in the world.?

_____

_____

_____

_____

_____

_____

❀ What can you do to insure you have the joy of the Lord in your daily life? How do you best connect with God? Through prayer? Time spent reading Scripture? Praise and worship music?

_____

_____

_____

_____

_____

_____

_____

❀ Have you ever been in the middle of a crazy, chaotic time yet still felt the overwhelming presence of a loving Savior?

_____

_____

_____

_____

_____

❀ What changes could you make in your life to better keep you balanced in your mind? In your soul? In your body? In your spirit?

_____

_____

_____

_____

Always Remember This –

God is always present in the calm and the chaos; it is up to you whether you acknowledge Him.

Prayer –

Father God, allow me to remember you are with me always. Let me rest in the comfort of knowing you are in control of my life. Teach me how to balance my life so that I will be better equipped and more empowered to pursue the path you have for me. Amen.

3

GOD HAS MADE US ALL UNIQUE AND SPECIAL

"...if my people, who are called by my name, will humble themselves and pray and seek my face and turn from their wicked ways, then I will hear from heaven, and I will forgive their sin and heal their land."

–2 Chronicles 7:14

Principles to Ponder –

- We all want to be free.
- The world views freedom differently than Christians do. As Christians, we want freedom but we want it under the security and safety of a heavenly Father. That is because we have seen the rebellion in our communities, our country, and around the world.
- God is the only one who can give true freedom and new life and gives it abundantly.

Questions to Discuss –

❋ How does the world's view of freedom differ from what Christians consider as freedom? What do you think nonbelievers want freedom from? How do they seek to secure it?

_____

_____

_____

_____

❋ What is your opinion regarding the women's marches for freedom throughout history? Do you think it is an effective way to bring about change?

_____

_____

_____

_____

❀ What does freedom in Christ mean to you personally?

_____

_____

_____

_____

_____

❀ What happens in your life and your relationship with
Christ when you humble yourself and pray earnestly to
God? Why is it so many believers turn to Christ as a
last resort rather than a first response?

_____

_____

_____

_____

_____

❀ Do you think the time is right in your community/
throughout our country/around the world for women to
wake up to their callings and embrace their God-given
divine assignments?

_____

_____

_____

_____

_____

_____

Always Remember This –

Regardless of what the world says, true freedom is found only in Christ.

Prayer –

Father God, teach me to better understand that I am free to be all that you have created me to be and to realize I am free to live with joy and purpose. Thank you that, when I call out to you, you forgive me and heal me. Help me to always remember: I am your daughter and I AM FREE. Amen.

WOMEN WHO WOKE UP IN THE BIBLE

"Cast your cares on the Lord and he will sustain you; he will never let the righteous be shaken."

–Psalm 55:22

Principles to Ponder –

- ❋ We all have an invitation to wake up to God's calling.
- ❋ The moment you decide to follow the good and perfect plan God has designed for you, your life is changed forever.
- ❋ The Bible is full of stories just like you—women who battled with self-worth, doubt, and insecurities; women who made poor choices but grew from them, and women who had others dependent upon them for so many needs.
- ❋ So many of the women of the Bible became honorable examples to learn from because of their decision to follow Christ.

Questions to Discuss –

- ❀ Read about Deborah's challenge in Judges, Chapter 4. What characteristics did she have that set her apart from most of the women of her day? Do you think you would have the same strength of character that she did when she led her people against their enemies?

_____

_____

_____

_____

_____

❀ Who, besides Deborah, helped to defeat the enemy for her country? Would you have been able to kill the remaining soldier to protect your country?

_____

_____

_____

❀ Read the story of the woman at the well in Samaria in the Book of John, Chapter 4. Can you identify with her hesitancy to break the cultural rules of her time or would you have been quick to offer aid? Have you experienced the life-giving benefits of the drink Christ was offering the woman?

_____

_____

_____

❀ Read the story of the woman caught in adultery in John, Chapter 8. What did Jesus say to the men bringing the accusation? What did he say to the woman? Have you ever felt personally targeted for a wrong decision? Have you ever maligned someone even while feeling the conviction of your own sin?

_____

_____

_____

Always Remember This –

Encouragement and inspiration to follow Christ, even in the most challenging of times, is never further away than a story from Scripture.

Prayer –

Father God, let me walk in your ways just as the women of the Bible did. Help me to learn from their examples and their faith. Show me your mercy and reveal your sacred plans to me. Help me to release my burdens to you and know that you will never lead me where you have not gone before me. Let me wake up every morning asking you to guide my steps, temper my tongue, and guard my thoughts. In doing so, I know my days will be covered with your grace. Amen.

Modern Day Sleeping Beauties

"'For I know the plans I have for
you,' declares the Lord,
"plans to prosper you and not to
harm you, plans to give you hope
and a future."

—Jeremiah 29:11

Principles to Ponder –

* There are many modern-day sleeping beauties— women who have awoken from a sleep of complacency and mediocrity to claim lives of dynamic service as godly examples for other women.
* It is encouraging to hear personal stories of awakening, renewal, and the impact of Christ upon women's lives.
* Women everywhere have a deep need for love, security, and significance.

Questions to Discuss –

❁ When you read the story of Chrissy Cymbala does it remind you of a time when you felt lost and hopeless? How did you move past the despair?

_____

_____

_____

❁ How does this story of love and forgiveness inspire you not to give up on you or others no matter the level of despair? Do you think her father was right in not allowing her to return home until she returned to her faith?

_____

_____

_____

❀ Would you have been able to humble yourself as Chrissy did and return home to ask for help?

_____

_____

_____

_____

❀ Do you believe in the power of intercessory power as was practiced on Chrissy's behalf? If not, what do you think motivated her to return home under her father's conditions?

_____

_____

_____

_____

❀ What did Chrissy eventually realize after her eyes were opened regarding the relationship she had previously been involved in?

_____

_____

_____

_____

Always remember –

No one's life is beyond restoration. With Christ, we all are given the chance for redemption.

Prayer –

Father God, help me to realize your overwhelming love and forgiveness—for me and for all who claim you. Teach me to hear your voice and graciously accept your plans for me for a hopeful and prosperous future. Help me never to forget that I can never stray beyond your forgiving grace. Amen.

6

GOD'S PLAN TO WAKE UP
SLEEPING BEAUTIES

"Before I was afflicted I went
astray, but now I obey your word.
You are good, and what you do is
good; teach me your decrees."

–Psalm 119:67-8

Principles to Ponder –

* Some people wake up easily and naturally; others have a harder time awakening. Some people respond at the first nudging; for others, it takes repeated wake up calls. This is true physically *and* spiritually.

* Different experiences and events cause us to wake. What may wake one sleeping beauty may not wake another. Again, this is true physically *and* spiritually.

* At different stages of your life, you may respond more readily than at times when you were less invested in the consequences of not awakening. Once again, this is true physically *and* spiritually.

Questions to Discuss –

❋ There are three primary ways God wakes us up. Can you identify them? Which method are you most responsive to? Has it always been this way or have different ways been more effective throughout your life?

_____

_____

_____

_____

_____

_____

_____

❀ How does God go about convicting our hearts? Your heart? Can you recall a time when God undeniably convicted your heart to hear his voice, change your course, and see his ways?

❀ Have you ever had a friend serve as a prophet to you and step in to waken you from spiritual sleep? Were you receptive or defensive? Have you ever been called by God to do the same for a loved one?

- Why is it so important for your heart to be repentive in order to fulfill your destiny in Christ? Is it a necessary ingredient for fellowship with Christ or can you skip this step and still enjoy a fruitful relationship with him?

Always Remember This –

It's not how many times we've sinned and fallen short of Christ's glory; it's how many times we turn back and receive Christ's mercy that matters.

Prayer –

Father God, I repent of my sins and failures. Open my heart to listen when you speak to me words of correction. I know that I walk in favor and I am a woman who is important to you and in the Kingdom of God. Let me have a tender heart and call out to you for help. Amen.

7

How God Can Wake You Up

"They triumphed over him
by the blood of the Lamb
and by the word of their
testimony; they did not love
their lives so much as to
shrink from death."

–Revelation 12:11

> " '...no weapon forged against you will prevail, and you will refute every tongue that accuses you. This is the heritage of the servants of the Lord, And this is their vindication from me,' declares the Lord."
>
> –Isaiah 54:17

Principles to Ponder –

* Everyone faces challenges—no one is exempt. However, what is important in terms of being a worthy Christian example is *how* you respond when challenges arise. While you can't always control the events of your life, you can *always* control how you respond to them.

* When you are known as a Christ-follower, people watch to see how you react to life's difficulties. For them, you may be the standard against which they measure how a believer handles setbacks. In other words, what you do and *how* you respond speaks much louder than anything you say.

Questions to Discuss –

❀ Read Daniel, Chapter 10. What vision did Daniel have when he prayed? Was he receptive to the challenge given to him or defiant? Did he understand what was happening as the vision occurred? Was it necessary for him to understand it completely before he was obedient to the Lord?

❀ Do you think there were demonic forces blocking his prayers? Why or why not?

❀ In the verse above (Revelation 12:11), how important

do you think it is to stand on the promises of Scripture when you are facing trials? Is it a natural response to seek out relevant Scripture when you face trouble or do you rely upon your own strength and wisdom?

※ In Acts, Chapter 10, an angel of the Lord appears to a centurion named Cornelius. The angel tells Cornelius that his "prayers and gifts to the poor have come up as a memorial offering before God." How important is it to you to give to others out of gratitude for what Christ has done for you? Do you maintain an ongoing prayer life with God or only turn to Him occasionally? What do you think the benefits of a continual, prayerful conversation with God would look like in your life?

Always Remember This –

No matter the challenge, we are called as believers to respond in a Christ-like manner and challenged to let God seek justice on our behalf.

Prayer –

Father God, I know I can face any battle as long as you are with me. You have promised never to leave or forsake me. Teach me to stand on your word and to speak words of faith in you whenever I am tested. Amen.

GOD'S PURPOSE FOR
SLEEPING BEAUTIES

" 'Have I not commanded you?
Be strong and courageous.
Do not be afraid; do not be
discouraged for the Lord your
God will be with you wherever
you go.' "

–Joshua 1:9

" 'And when you stand praying,
if you hold anything against
anyone, forgive them,
so that your Father in heaven may
forgive your sins.' "

–Mark 11:25

"Take delight in the Lord,
and he will give you the desires of
your heart."

–Psalm 37:4

Principles to Ponder –

* There is absolutely no one on the planet just like you. In so very many ways, you are a one-of-a-kind creation.

* God created you to have a purpose that is uniquely yours.

* Though others may appear to travel similar paths, have comparable talents and strengths, or share common personality traits, your God-designed purpose can be fulfilled by no one except you.

Questions to Discuss –

❀ Has fear ever stopped you from pursuing a dream? From trying new things? From risking an adventure? Have you ever stopped to consider what's the worst possible outcome and realize you could probably overcome it and, quite possibly, be stronger for it?

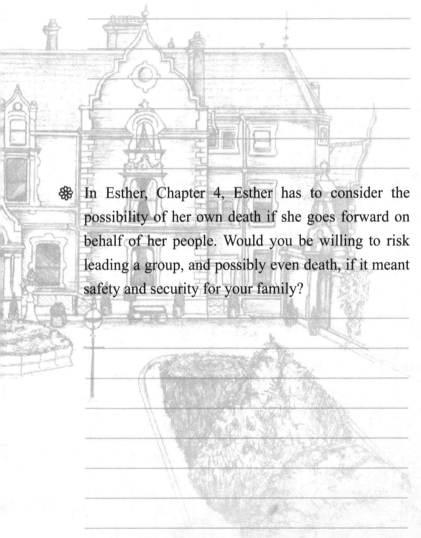

❀ In Esther, Chapter 4, Esther has to consider the possibility of her own death if she goes forward on behalf of her people. Would you be willing to risk leading a group, and possibly even death, if it meant safety and security for your family?

❀ Considering Esther's bravery and willingness to speak on her people's behalf, are you challenged to be bolder and stronger in living for Christ?

_____

_____

_____

_____

_____

_____

❀ Most of us don't routinely face the possibility of death just for taking a stand on a matter, but sometimes it seems just as threatening when our reputation, our integrity, or our name is on the line. Have you ever felt threatened on some level for standing on your convictions?

_____

_____

_____

_____

_____

_____

❀ All of us have been hurt and broken several, if not many, times throughout our lives. Why do you think it is important to see past the hurts and unkind words and actions and to forgive the offender and move beyond past mistakes?

_____

Always Remember This –

Delight in the Lord and forgive others as you have been forgiven by Christ.

Prayer –

Father God, help me to conquer the fears within me. Help me to always remember that if you are for me, no one can stand against me. Show me how to forgive the people who have hurt me in the past and help me to let go of anger. Teach me to delight myself in you and to always keep you front and center as Lord of my life. Amen.

9

SLEEPING BEAUTIES FROM AROUND THE WORLD

"If you fully obey the Lord your God and carefully follow all his commands I give you today, the Lord your God will set you high above all the nations on earth.

All these blessings will come on you and accompany you if you obey the Lord your God. You will be blessed in the city and blessed in the country."

–Deuteronomy 28:1-3

Principles to Ponder –

- There is a plan for your life. It is God-ordained, God-inspired, and God-driven. As a believer, you are called to allow Him to lead your journeys.
- When you obey God's direction for your life, He will awaken you to the plan He designed specifically for you.
- Once you awaken to God's call upon your life, you are able to help and awaken those around you.

Questions to Discuss –

- Have you ever heard God speak to you *deep within your spirit*? If so, what did He tell you? Did you act on what He shared?

_____

_____

❀ If you've heard the voice of God speak directly to you, have you considered writing down what was spoken to you? If not, try doing so and studying the words you received. Do you need to move beyond just hearing His words to doing something with what you've been told?

_____

_____

_____

_____

_____

❀ Can you look back and see how God has used past experiences and lessons learned to prepare you for the ministry available to you now? Have you suffered a miscarriage, endured a broken marriage, or raised a particularly challenging child that would allow you to share your journey with another woman going through this right now? Do you have insight into what you learned from your experience or words of hope and encouragement that you could offer to another hurting woman?

_____

_____

_____

❀ Have there been women in your life that have mentored you or helped you to develop a deeper relationship with God? How did they minister to you? What do you remember most about their involvement in your life?

_____

_____

_____

_____

_____

_____

_____

❀ Have you had the privilege of watching other women wake up to their true calling upon their life? What triggered the transformation? Could you help replicate it for other women?

_____

_____

_____

_____

_____

_____

Always Remember This –

Nothing is wasted with the Lord. All your steps have been ordered by God to be used for His glory.

Prayer –

Father God, I want to hear from you and fully embrace the calling you have for me. Teach me to dream again and show me how to achieve those dreams. God, I know everything in my life is to be used for what you have called me to do and that no experience is without cause. Today I confess I am 'all in' and ready to take the challenge to fully 'wake up' to your good and perfect will. Amen.

10

God Has a Master Plan for Sleeping Beauties

"Surely, Lord, you bless the
righteous; you surround them
with favor as a shield."

–Psalm 5:12

"But you, Lord, are a shield
around me, my glory,
the One who lifts my head high."

–Psalm 3:3

Principles to Ponder –

- There is security in knowing God has a divine master plan for your life even if you only catch a glimpse of your future now and then.
- You don't have to know all the 'hows' and 'whys' of fulfilling God's direction for your life; you need only know and trust Him.
- As a woman of God, you are called to trust that God is working all things out for your good and to take comfort in accepting He, alone, is God and we are not.

Questions to Discuss –

- In Genesis, Chapter 16, Hagar cries out, "You are the God who sees me…I have now seen the One who sees me." What were the circumstances for Hagar running from her mistress? Read the entire chapter. How was Hagar divinely redeemed?

_____

_____

_____

_____

_____

_____

❁ Consider this promise from Psalm 91:15-17:

> " 'Because he loves me,' says the Lord, 'I
> will rescue him; I will protect him, for he
> acknowledges my name. He will call on me,
> and I will answer him; I will be with him in
> trouble, I will deliver him and honor him.
> With long life I will satisfy him
> and show him my salvation.' "

❁ How can you be sure when you call out to the Lord
that He hears you? Do you ever doubt this promise
or question God's timing in response to your pleas?

_____

_____

_____

_____

❁ Read James 4:6. How does it explain the cause-and-
effect nature of repentance with grace and favor? Do
you regularly practice repentance when you know
you've sinned?

_____

_____

_____

_____

❈ Look again at Psalm 3:3 above. How is God *always* able to lift your head and your heart above your circumstances? Do you find it easy to doubt His willingness and abilities when life gets difficult? Do you ever consider yourself unworthy to even present your pleas before the Lord?

_____

_____

_____

_____

_____

❈ Rahab had a direct lineage to Jesus that could be traced generation-by-generation back to him. Though your ancestry may be a bit more complicated and lengthy, you can still trace your lineage to Christ once you become His daughter. Can you accept and embrace being a member of Christ's holy 'family tree?' Does knowing this empower you? Overwhelm you? Encourage you?

_____

_____

_____

_____

Always Remember This –

God sees you; God hears you; God covers you with grace and forgives your past, God surrounds you with favor.

Prayer –

Father God, I thank you, Lord, that you see me always; that you hear me always. I am grateful for the covering of grace, the forgiveness of my sins, and your eternal favor upon my life. I am able to walk through this life with my head held high because of your grace and mercy. Help me to understand that my life makes a difference and that generations can be changed because of my commitment to you. I rest in the comfort of your divine favor over my life. Amen.

11

A Dream Come True

"'Many women do noble things,
but you surpass them all.
Charm is deceptive, and beauty
does not last;
but a woman who fears the Lord
will be greatly praised.'"

–Proverbs 30:29-30

Principles to Ponder –

 ❋ God delights in giving us blessings beyond our wildest imagination. It brings Him joy to lavish the blessings of life upon His children.

 ❋ Many little girls are brought up believing in a fairy tale—life as a princess with a knight in shining armor and life in a castle. It can be a rude awakening when you realize that life is not as orderly and magical as it was for Sleeping Beauty, Cinderella, Snow White, and so on.

 ❋ Once you move fast the illusion of a fairy tale and commit to following Christ while pursuing your dreams, He will guide you down paths well beyond what you would dream a possibility.

Questions to Discuss –

 ❊ Did you buy into the fairy tale belief as a young girl? Did you dream of living in a castle with your very own Prince Charming? What was the turning point when you realized the fairy tale was a make-believe story and not 'real life?' How did you make adjustments from that point forward?

_____

_____

_____

_____

❀ Think back to the tale of Sleeping Beauty. When she fell asleep, her entire family fell asleep as did everyone else in the castle. In fact, the entire kingdom fell asleep when she slept. But when she awoke, so did everyone else—across the whole kingdom. Do you see the similarity between Sleeping Beauty awakening and the kingdom following suit *and* what can happen to those 'in your kingdom' when you become fully awake?

_____

_____

_____

❀ Your family, your community, country, and beyond are all waiting for you to wake up to Christ's call upon your life. You are a powerful force, full of knowledge and answers to the problems that plague so many others. You have within you the life-changing, eternity-giving answer to all of life's difficulties. What is holding you back from answering this call and helping others to receive this gift? If you knew you were protected and anointed to impact others, would you move forward?

_____

_____

_____

- Can you accept your appointment and authority as a royal daughter of the King? Can you help other women to accept this honorable ancestry? What could you do to help just one other woman to realize her 'royal worth' as the King's precious daughter? What about 10 women?

Always Remember This –

As Christ's own, you have been given the extraordinary privilege to change lives and bring others to Christ. Someone once shared Christ with you; now it is yours to share with others.

Prayer –

Father God, I ask you to give me the desires of my heart and the surprises, too! Help me to see myself as you see me—as a royal daughter of a might King. Please forgive my sins and wash me clean. Use the talents you've blessed me with to help me dream bigger than I've ever dared before. Wake me up to my destiny! Lord, show me your glory and allow me to have an encounter with you. Amen.

12

WOMEN OF INFLUENCE

" 'For if you remain silent at this
time, relief and deliverance for
the Jews will arise from another
place, but you and your father's
family will perish.
And who knows but that you
have come to your royal position
For such a time as this?' "

–Esther 4:14

Principles to Ponder –

* The world is full of ALL kinds of women—rich, poor, stay-at-home, full-time executive, and everyday women just like you. But however we may be different in how we look and how we spend our days, we all have needs and wants that can only be fulfilled when we allow God to awaken us to the life He designed for us.

* Women bring beauty and love to the world. Most of us have a natural desire to want to make our surroundings more inviting and more comfortable for those we love. Women traditionally bring a softness and a kinder, gentler presence wherever they go.

* Women wield tremendous power and influence over the next generation at home, in the workplace, in the community, and across the world. Though many women may not be as forceful as most men, nonetheless, a woman's presence cannot be understated for the impact it has upon others.

Questions to Discuss –

❀ What gifts are traditionally attributed to women and how they influence others? How are they different from traits frequently attributed to men? Do you consider one style of influence better than the other?

_____

_____

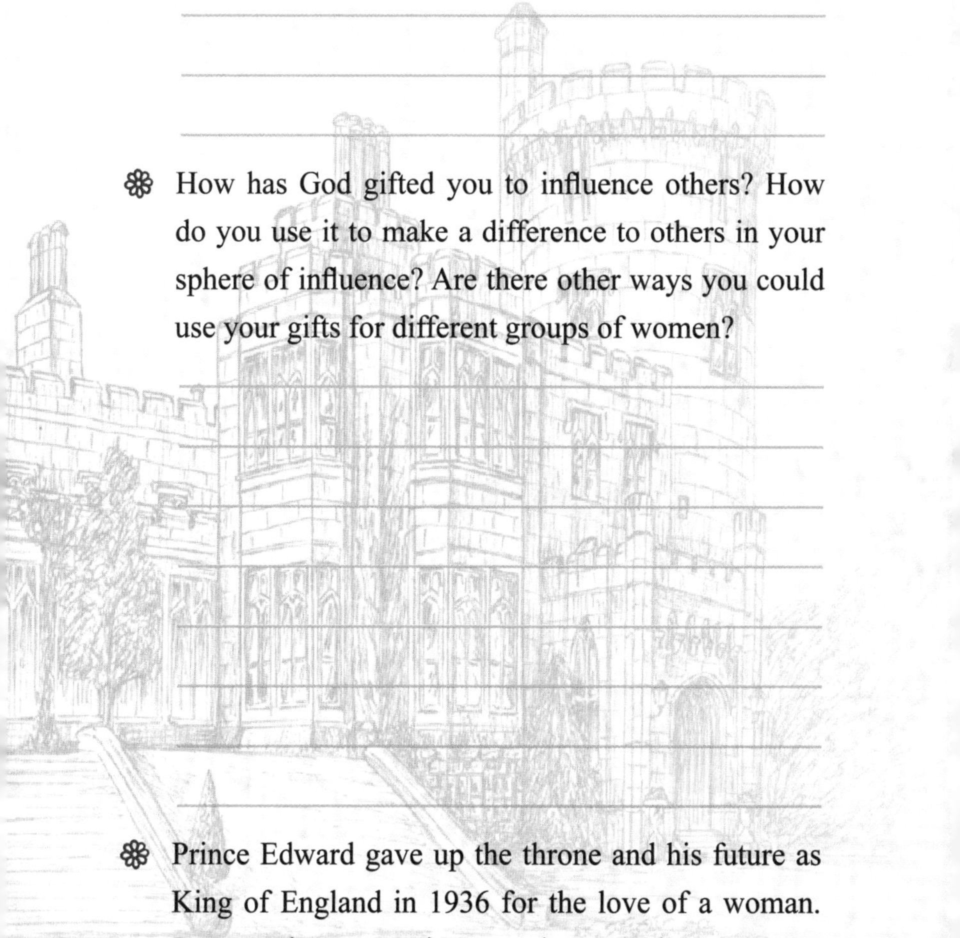

❀ How has God gifted you to influence others? How do you use it to make a difference to others in your sphere of influence? Are there other ways you could use your gifts for different groups of women?

❀ Prince Edward gave up the throne and his future as King of England in 1936 for the love of a woman. Because it was against royal protocol to marry a divorcee, he chose Wallis Simpson over life as a monarch. Though certainly a grand gesture of love, his actions also served to literally change the history of the world. Could you/would you allow a man to make such a sacrifice on your behalf? Have you ever felt loved to this degree?

_____

_____

_____

_____

_____

_____

_____

❋ Eighth-century Vikings were greatly influenced by the women of Scotland and Ireland. Even though it wasn't an organized and intentional effort to affect these rugged and unrefined men, the women's influence was undeniable and widespread. What was it about these women that so intrigued these men to the point of becoming kinder, gentler, and even considerably more civilized to win their favor? Have you seen this play out in modern day relationships?

_____

_____

_____

_____

❀ How can you intentionally use your presence and influence to wake up those around you? Do you have hopes of impacting a few in your near circle of friends and family or do you aspire to make a considerably larger impact? What would you need to do to be better equipped to influence more?

Always Remember This –

Never underestimate the power you have to affect change. In small and big ways alike, you are empowered to show Christ to the world.

Prayer –

Father God, I don't want an ordinary life. I want to wake up to my full potential and call upon every talent and gift you've given me. Wherever I am—home, office, community, or church—let me be full awake to your will. I want to use my voice and my influence for good over evil. You have given me wisdom, influence, beauty, and favor and I know that now is the time to step into my destiny, fully awake to your calling, and live for your glory. Amen.

To find out more about Judy Pogue and
Pogue Family Mission Society please visit:

JudyPogue.com